Theory and Sightreading for Singers

LEVEL 1
Second Edition

The EM Music
Voice Method Series

Written by

**Elizabeth Irene Hames
and Michelle Anne Blumsack**

Distributed by:

EM Music Publishing
2920 Yoakum St.
Fort Worth, TX 76108
EM.MusicPublishing@gmail.com

emmusicpublishing.com

Preface

This book provides a progressive curriculum for beginning theory and sightreading. It can be used in a classroom setting or as a complement to private study. The material is intended for middle-school aged students and older.

Each lesson provides instruction on theory, a worksheet to reinforce the concepts, and a sightreading exercise to provide practical application of those concepts. Each of the book's five units contains three lessons as well as a unit quiz. A downloadable answer key is available at www.emmusicpublishing.com under Our Books>Free Resources.

This second edition corrects minor errors and is fully compatible with the first edition.

Table of Contents

Unit 1

- Lesson 1: Notes and their Values I
- Lesson 2: The Staff and the Treble Clef
- Lesson 3: Measures and Time Signatures
- Unit 1 Quiz

Lesson 1
Notes and their Values I

Music notation tells a musician what pitches to play and how long to play them. Different symbols are used to show how long a note is to be held. **Rhythm** is the arrangement of long and short sounds.

A **quarter note** lasts for one beat:

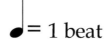 = 1 beat

A **half note** lasts for two beats:

 = 2 beats

A **whole note** lasts for four beats:

 = 4 beats

Most notes have a head and a stem.

The stem can either go up or down, making the note look like a "d" or a "p."

Did you know?
Written music has changed greatly over time.
A singer who lived 1,500 years ago would have read music that looked something like this.

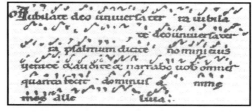

Worksheet 1
Notes and their Values I

1. Draw 4 quarter notes with stems going up:

2. Draw 4 quarter notes with stems going down:

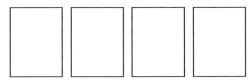

3. Draw 4 half notes with stems going up:

4. Draw 4 half notes with stems going down:

5. Draw 4 whole notes:

Solve these musical math problems:

1. ♩ + ♩ + ♩ = _____ beats

2. ♩ + ♩ + o = _____ beats

3. ♩ + ♩ + ♩ + o + ♩ = _____ beats

4. ♩ + o + ♩ + ♩ + o = _____ beats

Sightreading 1

Practice reading through the following exercises on "ta."

1.

2.

3.

4.

5.

Below, write your own rhythm exercise and read it aloud.

_____

Lesson 2
The Staff and the Treble Clef

In written music, a **staff** is a set of 5 lines and 4 spaces that hold the notes which tell us what to play or sing:

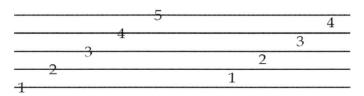

Notes located higher on the staff are higher in pitch, while notes located lower on the staff are lower in pitch.

In addition to lines and spaces, a staff will also have a **clef** that tells us which set of notes will be located on that staff. The first clef you will learn about is called the **treble clef**, also known as the "G" clef. It resembles a cursive "G":

The treble clef staff contains the notes sung by women and children, as well as higher pitched instruments, such as violin, flute, and oboe.

We use the letters A-G to give names to different notes. The line notes of the treble clef from lowest to highest are **E**, **G**, **B**, **D**, and **F**. You can remember their names by using the phrase "**E**very **G**ood **B**oy **D**oes **F**ine." The space notes of the treble clef spell out the word "**FACE**."

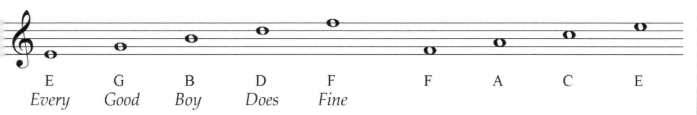

Notes can also be written above or below the staff. Two of these notes that you need to know now are **C** and **D**.

Notice that C has its own special line, which is called a **ledger line.**

Worksheet 2
The Staff and the Treble Clef

Complete the following sentences:

A staff is a set of _____ lines and_____ spaces which tells us what notes to play or sing.

The _____ clef, also known as the "G" clef, contains the notes sung by women and children, as well as many higher pitched instruments.

The line notes of the treble clef, from lowest to highest, are: ___, ___, ___, ___, and ___.

The space notes of the treble clef, from lowest to highest, are: ___, ___, ___, and ___.

On the staff below, draw 5 treble clefs.

Below each note, write its letter name.

Review
Next to each note, write the correct number of beats:

♩ = ___   ♩ = ___   o = ___

Sightreading 2

First, write the correct letter name below each note. Then read through each example in rhythm using the name of each note. Remember: Every Good Boy Does Fine and FACE.

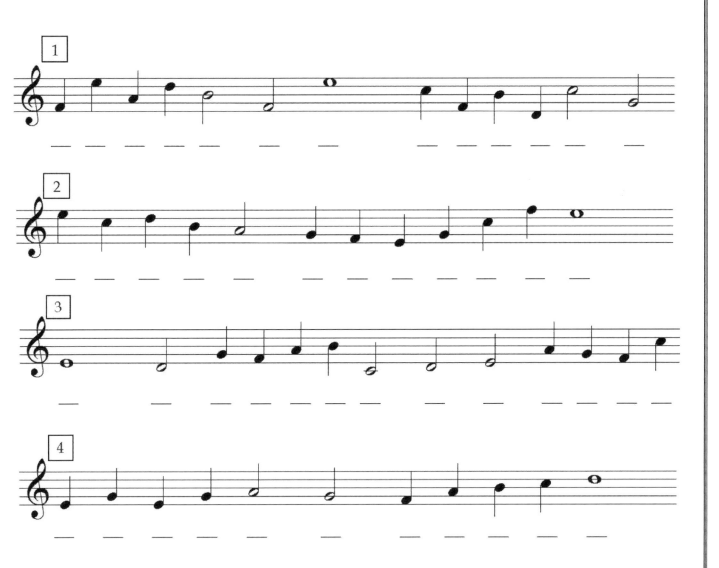

Lesson 3
Measures and Time Signatures

In music, notes are organized into **measures**, which can also be called **bars.** Measures are separated by **barlines** and contain a specific number of beats. A **double barline** is placed after the final measure of a piece to show that it is the end.

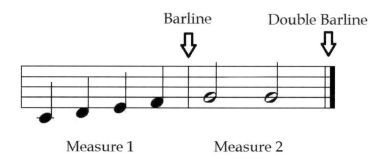

The number of beats in a measure is determined by the **time signature.** Time signatures are written with two numbers and look like a fraction. In most cases, the top number tells how many beats will be in a measure, and the bottom number tells what kind of note will get the beat. You can see how this works in the example below:

4 The top 4 shows that each measure will have 4 beats.

4 The bottom 4 shows that a quarter (or 1/4) note equals 1 beat.

Two other commonly used time signatures are 3/4 and 2/4. For both of these time signatures, the quarter note receives one beat, just like in 4/4 time. A measure in 3/4 time will have three beats while a measure in 2/4 time will have two beats.

Did you Know?
For now, you only need to worry about time signatures that have a "4" on the bottom, but there are many other time signatures you will learn about later, such as the ones listed below:

$$\frac{6}{8} \quad \frac{12}{8} \quad \frac{2}{2} \quad \frac{4}{2} \quad \frac{15}{16}$$

Worksheet 3
Measures and Time Signatures

1. How many beats per measure are in 4/4 time? _____

2. How many beats per measure are in 3/4 time? _____

3. How many beats per measure are in 2/4 time? _____

4. What type of note equals one beat in 3/4 time? _____

5. Write in the correct time signatures for the following examples:

6. Add barlines to divide the following example into measures, and add a double barline at the end.

<u>Sightreading 3</u>

Try clapping the following rhythms while counting the beats out loud as shown in the first two examples.

1.

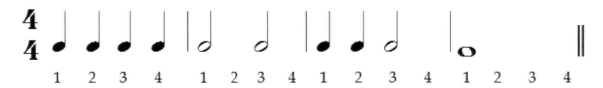

2.

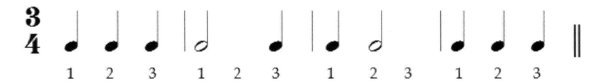

For the next two examples, write in the beats yourself and then clap and count the rhythms.

3.

4.

Unit 1 Quiz

Complete the following sentences:

A _____ note gets one beat, a _____ note gets two beats, and a _____ note gets four beats.

A _____ is a set of ____ lines and ____ spaces which tells us what notes to play or sing.

In music, notes are organized into _____, or bars, which are separated by _____ and contain a specific number of beats

A _____ _____ tells how many beats are in each measure.

Let's combine everything we have learned and write a song on the staff below, following all of the instructions carefully:

- **Step 1:** Draw a treble clef at the beginning of the staff.
- **Step 2:** Add a 4/4 time signature right after the treble clef.
- **Step 3:** Put the following notes in each measure.
  - **Measure 1:** E, D, C, D (all quarter notes)
  - **Measure 2:** E, E, E (quarter, quarter, half)
  - **Measure 3:** D, D, D (quarter, quarter, half)
  - **Measure 4:** E, G, G (quarter, quarter, half)
  - **Measure 5:** E, D, C, D (all quarter notes)
  - **Measure 6:** E, E, E (quarter, quarter, half)
  - **Measure 7:** D, D, E, D (all quarter notes)
  - **Measure 8:** C (whole note)
- **Step 4:** Finish the song by writing a double bar line at the end.

Bonus: What song is this? _____

Unit 2

- Lesson 4: Introduction to Solfege
- Lesson 5: Notes and their Values II
- Lesson 6: Steps and Skips
- Unit 2 Quiz

Lesson 4
Introduction to Solfege

In Lesson 2, we learned that notes have names which correspond with the first seven letters of the alphabet.

Unlike a pianist, who can find the right note on the keyboard and simply press it, a singer must know what note to sing before he sings it. Singers use **solfege** to help them learn the relationships between different pitches. Look at the ladder below. Notice that each syllable has a hand sign. Go through each syllable and sign with your teacher. Then sing the whole **scale**, or collection of pitches.

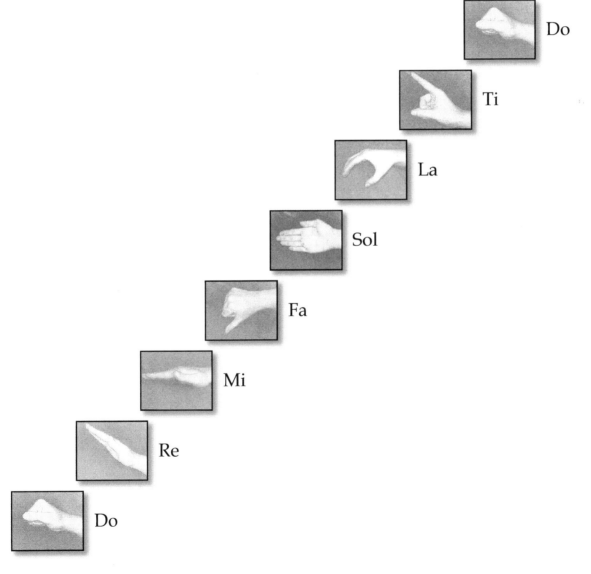

*Note that scales can start on any pitch. To begin, we will use the scale starting on C, where C is *Do*.*

13

Worksheet 4
Introduction to Solfege

1. What syllable is one note higher than *Do*? _____

2. What syllable is one note lower than *Fa*? _____

3. What syllable is two notes higher than *Mi*? _____

4. What syllable is two notes lower than *La*? _____

5. What syllable is two notes higher than *Ti*? _____

Underneath each note, write the correct letter name and the correct solfege syllable. Use the key to help you.

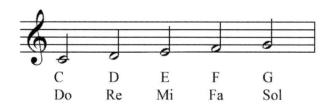

C	D	E	F	G
Do	Re	Mi	Fa	Sol

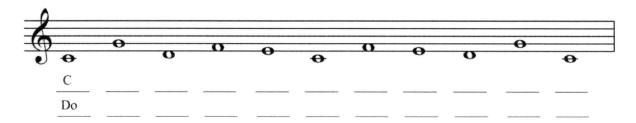

C
Do

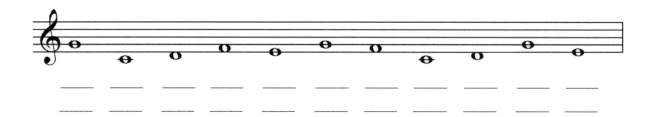

Sightreading 4

Underneath each pitch, write "D," "R," or "M" for the correct solfege syllable. Then, sign and speak each example in rhythm with your teacher. Finally, sign and sing.

Lesson 5
Notes and their Values II

In Lesson 1, we talked about quarter notes, half notes, and whole notes. These are just a few of the many types of notes found in music.

One of these other notes is called an **eighth note**, which receives half of a beat, meaning that there are two eighth notes in one beat. When counting using eighth notes, insert an + ("and") between beats to show the notes that occur between beats. An eighth note by itself looks like a quarter note with a flag. Two or more eighth notes can be joined together with a **beam.**

A dot can be added to any of the notes we have talked about to change its length. The dot adds half of the original value to the note. For example, a half note gets two beats. If a dot is added to the half note, making it a **dotted half note**, it will then have three beats.

$$\text{♩} = 2 \text{ beats} \quad 2 + 1/2 (2) = 3 \qquad \text{♩} + \bullet = \text{♩.} = 3 \text{ beats}$$

This formula can be used for any of the notes we have learned, resulting in the following note values:

o.	dotted whole note	4+2=6 beats
♩.	dotted half note	2+1=3 beats
♩.	dotted quarter note	1+½=1 ½ beats
♪.	dotted eighth note	½+¼=¾ beat

Did you know?
There are very simple mathematical relationships between all the different notes. Look at this figure to see how different note values relate to each other:

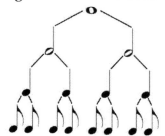

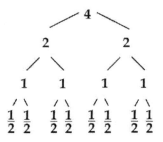

16

Worksheet 5
Notes and their Values II

Draw lines to match notes to the correct number of beats.

♩ (half note)   4 beats

♩ (quarter note)   1 beat

𝅝 (whole note)   1 ½ beats

♩. (dotted half note)   3 beats

♪ (eighth note)   2 beats

♩. (dotted quarter note)   ½ beat

Solve these musical math problems:

1. ♩. + ♩. + ♪ = ___ beats

2. 𝅝 + ♩. + ♩ = ___ beats

3. ♩. + ♪ + ♩. + 𝅝. = ___ beats

4. ♩. + 𝅝. + ♪ + ♪ + ♩ = ___ beats

On the staff below, label note names, solfege, and beats:

E _____

Mi _____

1 2 3 4 _____

Sightreading 5

Combine what you have learned about singing on solfege with the new rhythms from this lesson to sing the following melodies. Underneath each pitch, write "D," "R," or "M" for the correct solfege syllable. Then, sign and speak each example in rhythm with your teacher. Finally, sign and sing.

Lesson 6
Steps and Skips

Notes can move from one to the next in different ways. **Steps** and **skips** are the most basic types of musical movement.

A **step** occurs when one note moves to the one right next to it, either up or down. On the staff, a step moves from a line note to a space note or a space note to a line note:

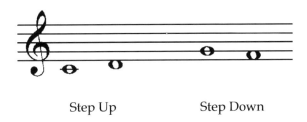

Step Up   Step Down

Steps are also called **2nds.**

A **skip** occurs when one note moves to another, skipping one or more notes in between. Skips can be small or large.

We will begin with the smallest type of skip, where we only skip one note. On the staff, this type of skip will have a line note moving to the nearest line note or a space note moving to the nearest space note.

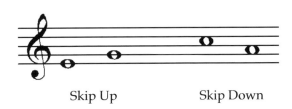

Skip Up   Skip Down

A skip where you only skip one note is called a **3rd.**

Worksheet 6
Steps and Skips

For each pair of notes, circle either 2nd (step) or 3rd (skip).

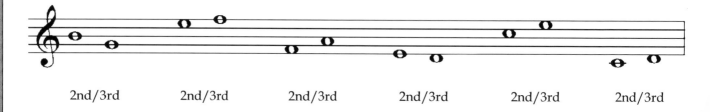

2nd/3rd   2nd/3rd   2nd/3rd   2nd/3rd   2nd/3rd   2nd/3rd

Next to each note, draw a whole note using the given distance and direction.

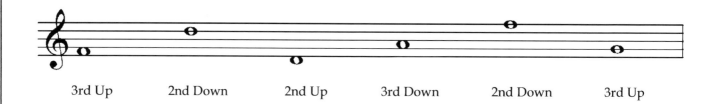

3rd Up   2nd Down   2nd Up   3rd Down   2nd Down   3rd Up

Both solfege and notes can move in 2nds and 3rds. Write the correct syllables or pitches below using the given distance and direction. Use the scales to help you.

Do Re Mi Fa Sol La Ti Do   C   D   E   F   G   A   B   C

1. A 2nd up from Mi is _____.   8. A 2nd up from C is _____.

2. A 3rd down from Sol is _____.   9. A 2nd down from F is _____.

3. A 2nd up from Fa is _____.   10. A 3rd up from D is _____.

4. A 3rd down from Ti is _____.   11. A 2nd up from G is _____.

5. A 2nd up from Sol is _____.   12. A 3rd down from A is _____.

6. A 3rd up from Do is _____.   13. A 2nd down from C is _____.

7. A 2nd up from Ti is _____.   14. A 3rd up from B is _____.

Sightreading 6

The sightreading examples below contain several skips. In each example, circle the skips and write "D," "R," "M," "F," or "S" for the correct solfege syllable. Then, sign and speak each example in rhythm with your teacher. Finally, sign and sing.

Do   Re   Mi   Fa   Sol

1

Do _____

2

Do _____

3

Do _____

Unit 2 Quiz

Complete the following sentences:

1. Singers use _____ (Do, Re, Mi, for example) to help them learn the relationships between different pitches.

2. A(n) _____ note receives half a beat. Two of these notes are often joined together by a _____.

3. A dotted half note receives _____ beats, since the dot adds half the value of the original note.

4. A(n) _____ occurs when one note moves to note right next to it. This is also called a(n) _____.

5. A(n) _____ occurs when one note moves to the next, passing over one or more notes. The smallest type is called a _____.

On the staff below, draw the notes indicated by the directions above the staff. Then go through and write the solfege and letter name for each note.

| 3rd Up | 2nd Down | 3rd Up | 2nd Up | 3rd Down | 3rd Down | 3rd Up | 3rd Up | 2nd Down | 2nd Down |

C

Do

| 3rd Down | 2nd Down | 3rd Up | 2nd Down | 3rd Up | 2nd Down | 3rd Down | 2nd Up | 2nd Down | 2nd Down |

Unit 3

- Lesson 7: Basic Dynamics
- Lesson 8: 4ths and 5ths
- Lesson 9: Rests
- Unit 3 Quiz

Lesson 7
Basic Dynamics

If you listen to a piece of music, you may notice that not everything is played at the same volume. Some pieces are quiet, other pieces are loud, and many move between quiet and loud throughout. This allows music to be more expressive and interesting. **Dynamics** is the term we use for how quiet or loud someone is playing or singing.

There are Italian terms for a wide range of dynamic levels, and each one has its own symbol used in music. Look at the table below to see some of the most common dynamics.

Dynamic Level	Italian Term	Symbol
very loud	*fortissimo*	*ff*
loud	*forte*	*f*
moderately loud	*mezzo forte*	*mf*
moderately quiet	*mezzo piano*	*mp*
quiet	*piano*	*p*
very quiet	*pianissimo*	*pp*

Did You Know?
You might wonder why the piano (the instrument) has the same name as the Italian term for quiet. This is because when the piano was invented, it was the first keyboard instrument that a musician could control the dynamics of simply by how hard he hit the keys. Because of this, the piano was originally called a "pianoforte," because it could easily play both *piano* and *forte*. Later, the name was shortened to "piano."

Worksheet 7
Basic Dynamics

Draw lines to match dynamic markings to the correct definition.

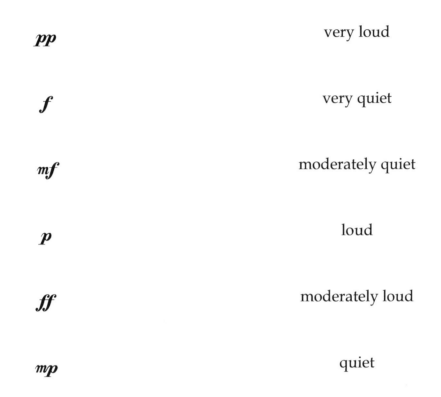

pp	very loud
f	very quiet
mf	moderately quiet
p	loud
ff	moderately loud
mp	quiet

For the following melodies, a) write in the correct time signature underneath the arrow, b) circle all 3rds, and c) add a dynamic marking in the box that you think fits the words.

Hush now ba - by; go to sleep. Rest in qui - et __ peace.

I will re - joice, __ for I __ am __ joy - ful.

Sightreading 7

Write in the solfege for each note, and then sing through the following melodies. Pay careful attention to the dynamics.

Do   Re   Mi   Fa   Sol

Lesson 8
4ths and 5ths

In Lesson 6, you learned that notes can move from one to the next in different ways, including steps and skips. An **interval** is the term musicians use to describe the distance between two notes. You have already learned the intervals of a **2nd** and **3rd.**

A **4th** is another type of skip. It skips over two notes and moves from a line note to a space note or a space note to a line note.

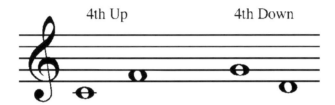

A 4th moving up sounds like the beginning of the song "Here Comes the Bride."

A **5th** is also a type of skip. It skips over three notes, and moves from a line note to a line note or a space note to a space note.

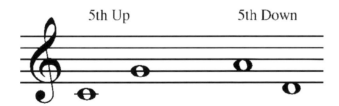

A 5th moving up sounds like the beginning of the song "Twinkle, Twinkle Little Star."

Worksheet 8
4ths and 5ths

For each pair of notes, circle either 4th or 5th.

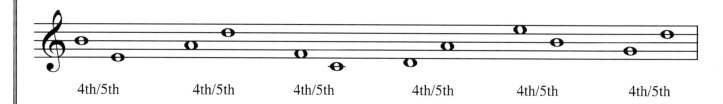

4th/5th   4th/5th   4th/5th   4th/5th   4th/5th   4th/5th

Next to each note, draw a whole note using the given distance and direction.

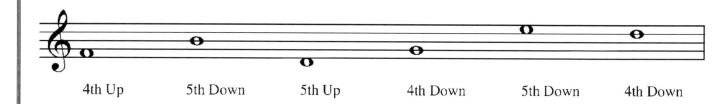

4th Up   5th Down   5th Up   4th Down   5th Down   4th Down

Write the correct syllables or pitches below using the given distance and direction. Use the scales to help you.

Do Re Mi Fa Sol La Ti Do   C   D   E   F   G   A   B   C

1. A 5th up from Mi is _____.   8. A 4th up from C is _____.

2. A 4th down from Sol is _____.   9. A 4th down from F is _____.

3. A 4th up from Fa is _____.   10. A 5th up from D is _____.

4. A 5th down from Ti is _____.   11. A 4th up from G is _____.

5. A 4th up from Sol is _____.   12. A 5th down from A is _____.

6. A 4th up from Do is _____.   13. A 4th down from C is _____.

7. A 5th up from Ti is _____.   14. A 5th up from B is _____.

Sightreading 8

In the following examples, you will be singing some new notes (La, Ti, and high Do).
Sing through the whole scale with your teacher first before singing the melodies.

Do   Re   Mi   Fa   So   La   Ti   Do

Do

Do

Do

The last example has some skips of 4ths and 5ths. Circle the 4ths and draw a box around the 5ths.

Do

Lesson 9
Rests

Our focus to this point has mainly been on notes, which tell you what pitches to play or sing and how long to hold them. In most pieces of music, however, the performer does not hold a note every single instant. Often there are beats or even measures at a time when the performer is silent. The sign used in music to show silence is the **rest.**

For each note we have learned about so far, there is a corresponding rest, which has its own symbol. The table below shows the most commonly used types of rests.

Name	Symbol	Duration	Note
Whole Rest	▬	4 Beats/1 Measure*	𝅝
Half Rest	▬	2 Beats	𝅗𝅥
Quarter Rest	𝄽	1 Beat	♩
Eighth Rest	𝄾	1/2 Half Beat	♪

* Unlike the whole note, the whole rest does not always last for four beats. It also is used to show a full measure of rest. If the time signature is 4/4, the whole rest will be four beats long. If the time signature is 2/4 or 3/4, the whole rest would last for two or three beats, respectively.

Tip: The whole rest and half rest look similar to each other and are easy to get mixed up. One way of keeping them straight is remembering that the **whole** rest looks like a **hole** in the ground, and the **half** rest looks like a **hat.**

Did You Know?
In many musical ensembles, the instrumentalists can have rests for a long time, sometimes even 100 measures or more. The musicians have to be sure to count carefully during their rests so that they come in at the right time when it is their turn to play.

Worksheet 9
Rests

| Whole Rest | Half Rest | Quarter Rest | Eighth Rest |

On the staves below, draw 8 of each type of rest using the image above as a guide.

Whole Rests

Half Rests

Quarter Rests

Eighth Rests

Add a rest at the end of each measure to give it the correct number of beats.

Sightreading 9

In the following examples, you will practice singing with rests. Make sure to be precise with the rests, cutting off at exactly the beginning of the rest.

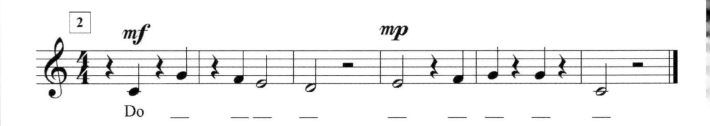

Unit 3 Quiz

Fill in the blanks in the table below.

Dynamic Level	Italian Term	Symbol
		mf
very quiet		
very loud		
	piano	
		mp
	forte	

Write a four measure melody using your choice of notes and rhythms. Be sure to do the following:

1) Add dynamics.
2) Include at least one skip of a 4th.
3) Include at least one skip of a 5th.
4) Include at least two different types of rests.
5) Label solfege.

Unit 4

- Lesson 10: Sharps and Flats
- Lesson 11: Key Signatures
- Lesson 12: Tempo
- Unit 4 Quiz

Lesson 10
Sharps and Flats

So far, we have talked about the notes in the musical alphabet (A,B,C,D,E,F,G). However, if you look at a piano keyboard, you will notice that there are some notes in between.

All the letters of the musical alphabet are on the white keys of the piano, but there are also black key notes. To play or sing the black key notes, we have to use **sharps** and **flats**. A sharp (#) raises a note by a half step, so if you played a C# on the piano, you would play the black key to the right of C. To sing a C#, you would find a note halfway between C and D. A flat (*b*) is the opposite of a sharp and lowers a note by a half step. For example on the piano, an E*b* would be the black key to the left of E, and for a singer, it would be a note halfway between E and D. Look at the piano keyboard below to see where the flats and sharps are.

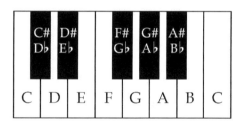

You may notice that the black keys can be called two different names. For example, F# and G*b* are the same note on the piano. When this happens, the notes are called **enharmonic**, meaning they share the same pitch and sound the same, but they have different names.

<u>Did You Know?</u>
You can also have sharps and flats that are white keys. Notice that E and B don't have black keys to the right, and F and C don't have black keys to the left. An E# is enharmonic to F, B# to C, F*b* to E, and C*b* to B.

Worksheet 10
Sharps and Flats

Fill in all the note names, including sharps and flats on the piano keyboard:

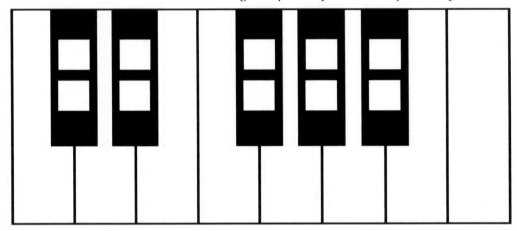

*Make all the notes below **sharp** and label the note name on the space below. Make sure that the sharp comes before the note and is on the same line or space as the note.*

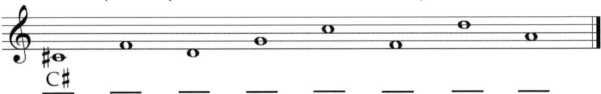

C#

*Make all the notes below **flat** and label the note name on the space below. Make sure that the sharp comes before the note and is on the same line or space as the note.*

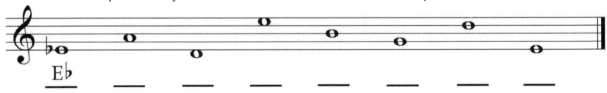

E♭

1. What note is enharmonic to C#? _____

2. What note is enharmonic to E♭? _____

3. What note is enharmonic to F#? _____

4. What note is enharmonic to G♭? _____

5. What note is enharmonic to A♭? _____

6. What note is enharmonic to D#? _____

Sightreading 10

The following examples demonstrate the use of sharps and flats. First you will sing a melody using only white notes. Then you will sing the same melody again with a sharp or flat added in. Remember that a sharp raises a note, and a flat lowers a note.

Notice that the solfege is altered slightly for sharps and flats. In this case, "Mi" will be lowered to "Me," and "Fa" will be raised to "Fi."

Do   Re   (Me)   Mi   Fa   (Fi)   So   La   Ti   Do

Lesson 11
Key Signatures

In Lesson 10, you learned that flats and sharps are used to notate the black notes on the piano. Flats and sharps help establish the **key** (or pitch center) of a piece of music. In terms of solfege, the key of a piece tells us where "Do" is. For example, in the key of C, C is "Do." In the key of G, G is "Do," etc.

Composers indicate the key by using a **key signature**, which is a collection of sharps or flats on the staff next to the clef. A key signature tells us which notes throughout that piece of music will be always "sharped" or "flatted."

The key signature below tells us that all the B's, E's and A's will be flatted.

This key signature tells us that all the F's, C's, G's and D's will be sharped.

To determine the key from a key signature, first determine whether the key is a "flat key" or a "sharp key." If there are no sharp or flats, the key is C.

For a flat key:
If the key signature has one flat, the key is "F." If the key has more than one flat, name the next to last flat.

Key of F   Key of Bb   Key of Eb   Key of Ab

For a sharp key:
Name the last sharp and go up one letter name.

Key of G   Key of D   Key of A   Key of E

Worksheet 11
Key Signatures

For each of the following "flat keys," circle the next to last flat (if applicable) and give the key.

Key: _____ _____ _____ _____ _____ _____

For each of the following "sharp keys," circle the last sharp. Then go up one letter to determine the key.

Key: _____ _____ _____ _____ _____

Keeping in mind that the key signature of a piece of music determines "Do," answer the following questions:

1. In the key of G:

    a. _____ is the letter name of the note "Do."

    b. The solfege for the note B is _____ .

    c. When you see the note _____ you should sing "Sol."

2. In the key of F:

    a. _____ is the letter name of the note "Do."

    b. The solfege for the note G is _____ .

    c. When you see the note _____ you should sing "La."

39

Sightreading 11

For each of the following examples, first determine the key. Then write the correct solfege beneath each note and sing through with your teacher.

1 Key of _____

Do _ _ _ _ _ _ _ _ _ _ _ _

2 Key of _____

Do _ _ _ _ _ _ _ _ _ _

3 Key of _____

Do _ _ _ _ _ _ _ _ _ _ _ _

4 Key of _____

Do _ _ _ _ _ _ _ _

Lesson 12
Tempo

The word **tempo** is used to describe how fast or slow a piece of music is. Often, composers will use **tempo markings** to indicate his desired pace. The following are some examples:

Tempo Marking	Meaning
Lento/Largo	Very Slowly
Adagio	Slowly
Andante	Walking Speed
Moderato	Moderately
Allegretto	Moderately Fast
Allegro	Quickly
Vivace	Lively and Fast
Presto	Very Fast

To practice maintaining a consistent tempo, musicians employ the use of a **metronome**, a device which produces a steady click. Composers will often include a **metronome marking**, which shows how many beats will be in one minute. For example, if you see the marking on the left, you will sing or play one quarter note each second, since there are 60 seconds in a minute. The marking on the right shows a faster tempo. In this case, there would be two quarter notes per second.

$$\text{♩} = 60 \qquad\qquad \text{♩} = 120$$

Did You Know?

Tempos will feel fast or slow depending on their relationship to your heartbeat. Most people's hearts beat around 60-70 times per minute. Because of this, a tempo faster than 70 beats per minute (**bpm**) will feel fast, and a tempo slower than 60 bpm will feel slow.

Worksheet 12
Tempo

Define the following tempo markings:

1. *Lento/Largo* _____

2. *Allegro* _____

3. *Moderato* _____

4. *Vivace* _____

5. *Adagio* _____

6. *Andante* _____

7. *Allegretto* _____

8. *Presto* _____

For each of the following examples, choose a tempo marking that would appropriately express the mood:

1. A mother is rocking her baby to sleep. _____

2. A cartoon in which a wolf is chasing a rabbit. _____

3. A man and a woman having a picnic in a park. _____

4. A group of people country line dancing. _____

5. A student walking to the principal's office. _____

6. A military march. _____

7. A 100 meter dash. _____

8. A student finishing his worksheet before class ends. _____

Sightreading 12

Label the key for each of the following examples. As you sing, be sure to pay attention to the tempo markings. From now on, try to sing the correct solfege without writing it in first.

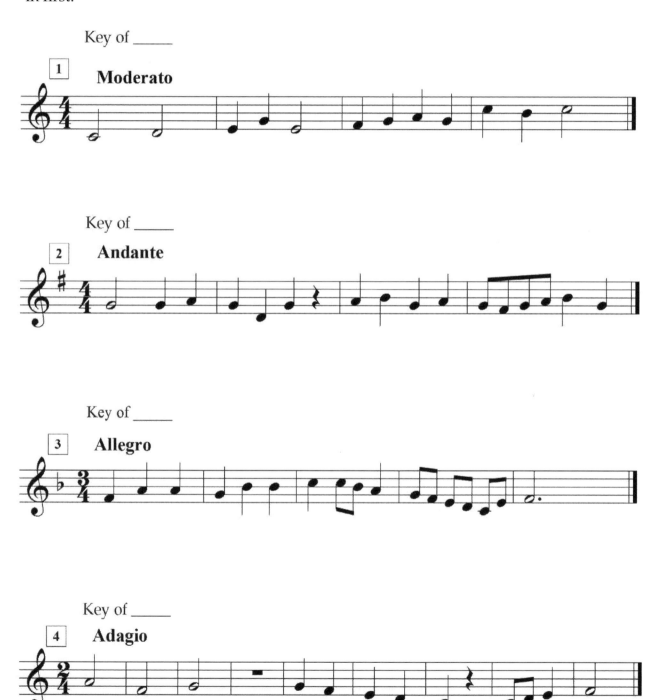

Unit 4 Quiz

Complete the following sentences:

1. A _____ is a symbol that raises a note by a half step.

2. A_____ is a symbol that lowers a note by a half step.

3. The enharmonic pitch of E♭ is _____ .

4. The enharmonic pitch of G# is _____ .

5. The _____ _____ is a set of sharps or flats that helps establish the pitch center (Do) of a piece of music.

6. The _____ describes how fast or slow a piece of music should be. *Lento* means _____ while *presto* means _____ .

Determine the key for the example below. Then write the correct solfege below each note.

Key of _____

Bonus On the staff below, determine the key, and write the same melody used in the example above in the new key.

Key of _____

Unit 5

- Lesson 13: Bass Clef
- Lesson 14: Musical Articulation
- Lesson 15: Unison vs. Harmony
- Unit 5 Quiz

Lesson 13
Bass Clef

In Lesson 2, you learned that a staff is a collection of 5 lines and 4 spaces which hold the notes that tell us what to play or sing. You also learned that a clef tells us what set of notes will be on that staff.

So far, everything you have seen has been written in the treble clef. The next clef you will learn is called the **bass clef**, also known as the "F" clef, because it used to look like a cursive F.

The bass clef staff contains the notes sung by men whose voices have changed, as well as lower pitched instruments, such as the tuba, bassoon and cello.

The line notes of the bass clef from lowest to highest are **G**, **B**, **D**, **F**, and **A**. You can remember their names by using the phrase "**Great Big Dogs Fight Animals**." The space notes of the bass clef from lowest to highest are **A**, **C**, **E**, and **G**. You can remember their names by using the phrase **All Cows Eat Grass**.

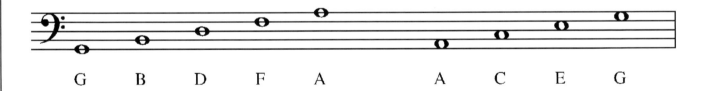

As you learned in Lesson 2, notes can be written above or below the staff. Two of those notes that you will see frequently are middle C (notice its ledger line; this is the same C that lives below the treble clef) and the B below it.

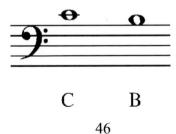

46

Worksheet 13
Bass Clef

Complete the following sentences:

The _____ clef, also known as the "F" clef, contains the notes sung by men, as well as many lower pitched instruments.

The line notes of the bass clef, from lowest to highest, are: ___, ___, ___, ___, and ___.

The space notes of the bass clef, from lowest to highest, are: ___, ___, ___, and ___.

On the staff below, draw 5 more bass clefs. Note the placement of the dots around the "F" line.

Below each note, write the correct letter name.

Sightreading 13

Each of the following examples is written using the bass clef. First determine the key for each example then sing through with your teacher.

1   Key of _____

2   Key of _____

3   Key of _____

4   Key of _____

Lesson 14
Musical Articulation

It was mentioned in Lesson 7 that there are more aspects to music than just notes and rhythms. You learned about different dynamics, which tell you how loud or soft to play. Another aspect of music is **articulation**, which tells you how a note or a group of notes is to be played or sung.

One of the most basic articulations in music is the idea of **legato**. Legato is an Italian term meaning smooth and connected. When you sing a legato musical line, you should move seamlessly from one note to the next without any pause or break in between. The marking used to show legato is a curved line called a **slur**.

As you can see in the example above, slurs can be placed over two or more notes at a time. The group of notes under each slur should be played or sung legato. Between slurs, the performer should give a small lift or take a quick breath. The idea of lifting between slurs is called phrasing. In vocal music, a slur is also used to show that a syllable is to be held through multiple notes.

In addition to slurs, many other types of articulations are found in pieces of music. The table below shows some of the most common markings that you might encounter.

Marking	Term	How to Sing
	Staccato	Short and separated (Opposite of legato)
	Accent	Louder than surrounding notes. Imagine you are "hitting" this note harder than the rest.
	Tenuto*	This marking can have many meanings. In singing, it usually means to give the note special emphasis.
	Fermata	Hold the note longer than its normal value. It can be held a little bit longer or much longer.

Worksheet 14
Musical Articulation

1) *Add articulation markings to the following melodies that fit the words.*
   Note*: You can use more than one type of marking per example, and it is not necessary to put a marking on every note.*

2) *Label letter names and solfege syllables for each note underneath the words.*

Pit - ter pat - ter, rain-drops fal - ling on my head to - day.

G

Sol

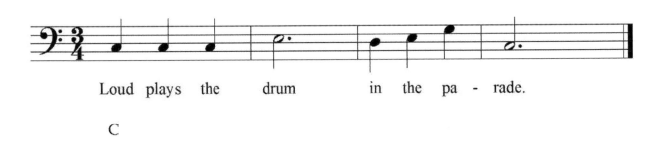

Loud plays the   drum   in the pa - rade.

C

Do

Sail - ing through the glas-sy sea. What fine wea-ther we have to - day.

C

Do

Sightreading 14

Each of the following contains various articulations which will impact the way certain notes are sung. For each example, determine the key and sing through with your teacher, taking note of the articulations.

Lesson 15
Unison vs. Harmony

So far everything we have talked about has only had a single musical line. When two or more people sing the same notes at the same time, we say they are in **unison**. You have probably noticed in music you hear that much of the time, there are multiple parts at the same time. A piece might have two people singing different notes plus a piano that is playing its own part. Even though the different performers are not playing and singing the same thing, everything fits together and sounds good. This is an example of **harmony**.

In previous lessons, we have talked about the intervals of the 2nd, 3rd, 4th, and 5th. For each of these intervals, there are two types: **melodic intervals**, where the notes are played separately, and **harmonic intervals**, where the notes are played at the same time. When two people are singing different parts at the same time, harmonic intervals occur between the two parts.

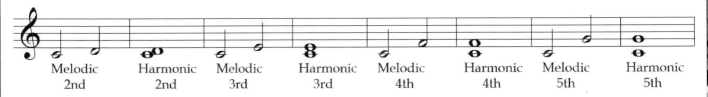

Melodic 2nd | Harmonic 2nd | Melodic 3rd | Harmonic 3rd | Melodic 4th | Harmonic 4th | Melodic 5th | Harmonic 5th

There are many rules in music for how to put parts together and create good harmony. We will explore this more in the Level 2 book of Theory and Sightreading for Singers.

Did You Know?
When music first began to be written down, it was in only one part, known as *monophony*. It was a great innovation when composers began to write *polyphony*, music involving multiple independent lines. Polyphony started to become popular at the end of the Middle Ages and was explored deeply during the Renaissance era, which lasted around the years 1400-1600. With each successive era of music history, composers found new and exciting ways to weave parts together and create beautiful harmony.

Worksheet 15
Unison vs. Harmony

Label the following intervals, and identify as harmonic (H) or melodic (M.)

M-3 _____ _____ _____ _____ _____ _____ _____ _____

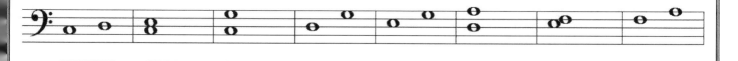

_____ _____ _____ _____ _____ _____ _____

Label the intervals between the two lines.

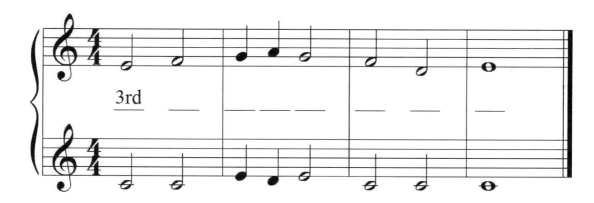

3rd _____ _____ _____ _____ _____

Write your own harmony to go with the following line. There are no right or wrong answers, but 3rds, 4ths, and 5ths will work better than 2nds in most cases.

Sightreading 15

The following examples demonstrate singing in two-part harmony. Sing through each line separately with your teacher and then try to sing the two parts together.

Unit 5 Quiz

Draw each of the indicated pitches on the staff using whole notes.

C   E   G   F   D   B   A   C   D   G   F   E

Complete the chart below.

Marking	Term	How to Sing
	Staccato	
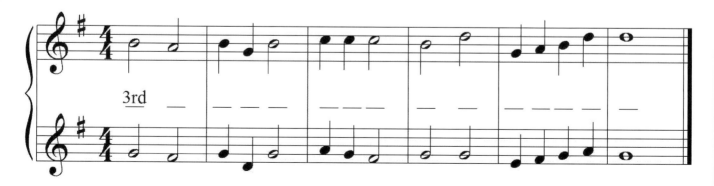		
		This marking can have many meanings. In singing, it usually means to give the note special emphasis.
	Fermata	

Label the intervals between the two lines.

3rd ___ ___ ___ ___ ___ ___ ___ ___ ___ ___ ___

Final Review

1. A _____ is a set of 5 lines and____ spaces which tells us what notes to play or sing.

2. The _____ clef, also known as the _____ clef, contains the notes sung by women and children, as well as many higher pitched instruments.

3. The line notes of the treble clef, from lowest to highest, are: ___, ___, ___, ___, and ___.

4. The space notes of the treble clef, from lowest to highest, are: ___, ___, ___, and ___.

5. The _____ clef, also known as the _____ clef, contains the notes sung by men, as well as many lower pitched instruments.

6. The line notes of the bass clef, from lowest to highest, are: ___, ___, ___, ___, and ___.

7. The space notes of the bass clef, from lowest to highest, are: ___, ___, ___, and ___.

8. A _____ _____ tells how many beats are in each measure.

9. In 4/4 time, there will be _____ beats per measure.

10. In 2/4 time, there will be _____ beats per measure.

11. In 3/4 time, there will be _____ beats per measure.

12. In music, notes are organized into _____, or bars, which are separated by _____ and contain a specific number of beats

13. Singers use _____ (Do, Re, Mi, for example) to help them learn the relationships between different pitches.

14. A _____ is a symbol that raises a note by a half step.

15. A _____ is a symbol that lowers a note by a half step.

16. The _____ _____ is a set of sharps or flats that helps establish the pitch center (Do) of a piece of music.

17. The _____ describes how fast or slow a piece of music should be. *Lento* means _____ while *presto* means _____

Match each item on the left to its definition on the right.

1. ♩ >

                             a. One Beat

2. **Andante**

                             b. Staccato

3. 𝅗𝅥.

                             c. Quickly

4. ♪

                             d. Three Beats

5. 𝄾

                           e. Two Beats of Silence

                           f. Accent Mark

6. **Allegro**

                           g. Half Beat of Silence

7. ♩̆

                           h. Fermata

8. *f*

                           i. Very Slowly

9. ▬

                           j. Moderately Quiet

10. **Largo**

                           k. Very Quiet

11. *mp*

                           l. Half of a Beat

12. *pp*

                           m. Loud

13. ♩

                           n. One Beat of Silence

14. 𝄽

                           o. Walking Speed

15. ♩̣

Use the directions below, which will guide you through a well-known tune.

Measure 1: (all quarter notes)
- Start on Do.
- Repeat Do.
- Write a note up a fifth from Do.
- Repeat that note.

Measure 2: (quarter, quarter, half)
- Start on La.
- Repeat La.
- Write a note down a second from La.

Measure 3: (all quarter notes)
- Start on Fa.
- Repeat Fa.
- Write a note a step down from Fa.
- Repeat that note.

Measure 4: (quarter, quarter, half)
- Start on Re.
- Repeat Re.
- Write a note a step down from Re.

Measure 5: (all quarter notes)
- Start a fifth up from Do.
- Repeat that note.
- Write a note a fourth up from Do.
- Repeat that note.

Measure 6: (quarter, quarter, half)
- Start on Mi.
- Repeat Mi.
- Write a note a step down from Mi.

Measures 7-8: Repeat measures 5-6.
Measures 9-12: Repeat measures 1-4.

Key of _____

Bonus What song is this? _____

58

Glossary

2nd- movement from one note to the note right next to it, either up or down, also called a **step**. (Lesson 6)

3rd- movement from one note to another skipping exactly one note. (Lesson 6)

4th- movement from one note to another skipping two notes. (Lesson 8)

5th- movement from one note to another skipping three notes. (Lesson 8)

Accent- a symbol showing that a note is to be played louder than the surrounding notes. (Lesson 14)

Adagio- slowly. (Lesson 12)

Allegretto- moderately fast. (Lesson 12)

Allegro- quickly. (Lesson 12)

Andante- walking speed. (Lesson 12)

Articulation- a symbol used to inform a musician how a note or group of notes is to be played or sung. (Lesson 14)

Bar-- a group of notes containing a fixed number of beats. Also known as a **measure**. (Lesson 3)

Barline- a vertical line used to separate measures. (Lesson 3)

Bass Clef- the clef used for lower pitched notes, also known as the "F" clef. (Lesson 13)

Beam- a horizontal line that joins together two or more eighth notes. (Lesson 5)

BPM- beats per minute. (Lesson 12)

Clef- a symbol that tells which set of notes will be located on a given staff. (Lesson 2)

Dotted Half Note- a note that lasts for three beats. (Lesson 5)

Dotted Quarter Note- a note that lasts for one and a half beats. (Lesson 5)

Double barline-a symbol placed after the final measure of a piece to show that it is the end. (Lesson 3)

Dynamics-terms that describe volume in music. (Lesson 7)

Eighth Note-a note that lasts for half of a beat. (Lesson 5)

Eighth Rest-one half beat of silence. (Lesson 9)

Enharmonic-a term used to describe notes that have the same pitch but are written differently. (Lesson 10)

Fermata-a symbol showing that a note is to be held longer than its normal value. (Lesson 14)

Flat-a symbol used to lower a note by a half step. (Lesson 10)

Forte-loud. (Lesson 7)

Fortissimo-very loud. (Lesson 7)

Half Note-a note that lasts for two beats. (Lesson 1)

Half Rest-two beats of silence. (Lesson 9)

Harmonic Interval-two notes played together. (Lesson 15)

Harmony-the combination of two or more notes resulting in a pleasant sound. (Lesson 15)

Interval-the distance between two notes. (Lesson 8)

Key-pitch center. (Lesson 11)

Key Signature-set of sharps or flats that denotes the key. (Lesson 11)

Largo-very slowly. (Lesson 12)

Ledger Line-a special line used for notes written below or above the staff. (Lesson 2)

Legato-smooth and connected. (Lesson 14)

Lento-very slowly. (Lesson 12)

Melodic Interval-two notes played separately. (Lesson 15)

Metronome Marking-shows exact tempo by denoting the number of beats per minute. (Lesson 12)

Measure-a group of notes containing a fixed number of beats. Also known as a **bar**. (Lesson 3)

Metronome-a device used to help musicians maintain a steady tempo. (Lesson 12)

Mezzo Forte-moderately loud. (Lesson 7)

Mezzo Piano-moderately quiet. (Lesson 7)

Moderato-moderately. (Lesson 12)

Pianissimo-very quiet. (Lesson 7)

Piano-quiet. (Lesson 7)

Presto-very fast. (Lesson 12)

Quarter Note-a note that lasts for one beat. (Lesson 1)

Quarter Rest-one beat of silence. (Lesson 9)

Rest-the sign used in music to show silence. (Lesson 9)

Rhythm-the arrangement of long and short sounds. (Lesson 1)

Scale-collection of pitches. (Lesson 4)

Sharp-a symbol used to raise a note by a half step. (Lesson 10)

Skip-movement from one note to another, skipping one or more notes in between. (Lesson 6)

Slur-a curved line used to show that notes are to be played smoothly and connected. (Lesson 14)

Solfege-syllables used to help singers learn note relationships. (Lesson 4)

Staccato-short and separated. (Lesson 14)

Staff-a set of 5 lines and 4 spaces that hold the notes which tell us what to play or sing. (Lesson 2)

Step-movement from one note to the note right next to it, either up or down, also called a **2nd**. (Lesson 6)

Tempo-the speed of a piece of music. (Lesson 12)

Tempo Markings-words used to describe the speed of a piece of music. (Lesson 12)

Tenuto-a marking that can have many meanings. In vocal music, it usually means to give the note special emphasis. (Lesson 14)

Time Signature-two numbers used to show how many beats per measure. (Lesson 3)

Treble Clef-the clef used for higher pitched notes, also known as the "G" clef. (Lesson 2)

Unison-when two or more musicians play or sing the same notes at the same time. (Lesson 15)

Vivace-lively and fast. (Lesson 12)

Whole Note-a note that lasts for four beats. (Lesson 1)

Whole Rest-four beats or a whole measure of silence. (Lesson 9)